Tru

by Jay Presson Allen

From the Words and Works of
Truman Capote

A Samuel French Acting Edition

SAMUELFRENCH.COM

Copyright © 2013 by Jay Presson Allen

ALL RIGHTS RESERVED

CAUTION: Professionals and amateurs are hereby warned that *TRU* is subject to a licensing fee. It is fully protected under the copyright laws of the United States of America, the British Commonwealth, including Canada, and all other countries of the Copyright Union. All rights, including professional, amateur, motion picture, recitation, lecturing, public reading, radio broadcasting, television and the rights of translation into foreign languages are strictly reserved. In its present form the play is dedicated to the reading public only.

The amateur and professional live stage performance rights to *TRU* are controlled exclusively by Samuel French, Inc., and licensing arrangements and performance licenses must be secured well in advance of presentation. PLEASE NOTE that amateur licensing fees are set upon application in accordance with your producing circumstances. When applying for a licensing quotation and a performance license please give us the number of performances intended, dates of production, your seating capacity and admission fee. Licensing fees are payable one week before the opening performance of the play to Samuel French, Inc., at 45 W. 25th Street, New York, NY 10010.

Licensing fee of the required amount must be paid whether the play is presented for charity or gain and whether or not admission is charged.

Professional/Stock licensing fees quoted upon application to Samuel French, Inc.

For all other rights than those stipulated above, apply to: International Creative Management, 730 Fifth Avenue, New York, NY 10019; attn: Buddy Thomas.

Particular emphasis is laid on the question of amateur or professional readings, permission and terms for which must be secured in writing from Samuel French, Inc.

Copying from this book in whole or in part is strictly forbidden by law, and the right of performance is not transferable.

Whenever the play is produced the following notice must appear on all programs, printing and advertising for the play: "Produced by special arrangement with Samuel French, Inc."

Due authorship credit must be given on all programs, printing and advertising for the play.

ISBN 978-0-573-70034-7   Printed in U.S.A.   #28021

No one shall commit or authorize any act or omission by which the copyright of, or the right to copyright, this play may be impaired.

No one shall make any changes in this play for the purpose of production.

Publication of this play does not imply availability for performance. Both amateurs and professionals considering a production are strongly advised in their own interests to apply to Samuel French, Inc., for written permission before starting rehearsals, advertising, or booking a theatre.

No part of this book may be reproduced, stored in a retrieval system, or transmitted in any form, by any means, now known or yet to be invented, including mechanical, electronic, photocopying, recording, videotaping, or otherwise, without the prior written permission of the publisher.

MUSIC USE NOTE

Licensees are solely responsible for obtaining formal written permission from copyright owners to use copyrighted music in the performance of this play and are strongly cautioned to do so. If no such permission is obtained by the licensee, then the licensee must use only original music that the licensee owns and controls. Licensees are solely responsible and liable for all music clearances and shall indemnify the copyright owners of the play and their licensing agent, Samuel French, Inc., against any costs, expenses, losses and liabilities arising from the use of music by licensees.

IMPORTANT BILLING AND CREDIT REQUIREMENTS

All producers of *TRU must* give credit to the Author of the Play in all programs distributed in connection with performances of the Play, and in all instances in which the title of the Play appears for the purposes of advertising, publicizing or otherwise exploiting the Play and/or a production. The name of the Author *must* appear on a separate line on which no other name appears, immediately following the title and *must* appear in size of type not less than fifty percent of the size of the title type.

In addition the following credit *must* be given in all programs and publicity information distributed in association with this piece:

The Estate shall receive billing credit as follows:

From the Words and Works of Truman Capote

Said credit shall appear on a separate line, immediately following the credit accorded Jay Presson Allen, as author. Said credit shall appear wherever the author's credit appears except for ABC, teaser and critics' quote ads. The name "Truman Capote" shall be 66-2/3% percent of the size of the author's credit.

There will also be a program credit substantially as follows:

TRU is being presented by special arrangement with the Estate of Truman Capote, Alan U. Schwartz, Executor

TRU was first presented on Broadway, on December 14, 1989, at the Booth Theatre in New York City, by Lewis Allen, David Brown, Suntory International Corporation, and The Shubert Organization, in association with The Landmark Entertainment Group, by arrangement with The Truman Capote Estate. The sets were designed by David Mitchell, with costume design by Sarah Edwards, lighting by Ken Billington and Jason Kantrowitz, sound design by Otts Munderloh, make-up design by Kevin Haney, wig design by Paul Huntley, general management by Stuart Thompson, production stage management by Ruth Kreshka, and stage management by Jane Grey. The director was Jay Presson Allen. The cast was as follows:

TRUMAN CAPOTE .... Robert Morse
VOICE OF JAN .... Jayne Atkinson
VOICE OF TELEPHONE OPERATOR .... Jill Choder
VOICE OF MRS. FERGUSON .... Sarah Schiff
VOICE OF SECRETARY......................... Jeanne Tripplehorn

CHARACTERS

TRUMAN CAPOTE
VOICE OF JAN
VOICE OF TELEPHONE OPERATOR
VOICE OF MRS. FERGUSON
VOICE OF SECRETARY

ACT 1

(On the curtain is an enormous blowup of the November 1975 issue of Esquire *magazine. It is a photograph of Truman Capote who teasingly regards the viewer from under a big black hat… in his hand a dagger, the sharp and shiny blade of which is tipping the hat's brim in a sly salute. The hat, the trenchcoat, the unsheathed knife imply that here is a spy, a man of dangerous secrets. His expression implies that he might …out of sheer mischief …reveal those secrets.)*

(The curtain remains down as the sound of Louis Armstrong's A Kiss to Build a Dream On* *comes up. Armstrong sings several bars before we hear a phone ringing. It rings three times, then the volume is turned down on the music. Phone rings once more before it is answered.)*

TRUMAN'S VOICE. *(recorded)* Yee-eesss?…Sugar? Where have you been? These days when someone doesn't call me right back I tend to get a trifle…agitated?…Oh day before yesterday. On the redeye …A last minute booking on *The Today Show.* Oh, just to fire a warning shot, let them know I'm back in town. Armed and dangerous. *(laughs)* So what's up? Anything happening to anybody besides me? Have you seen the Spook?…He has?…He did?…And she was with him? Whenever I see those two together I ask myself one question. What do they do? I believe they have invented a new vice. In what it consists I dare not guess.

(The curtain rises.)

(live) …but I believe…

---

*See Music Use Note on page 3.

*(We see **TRUMAN** on a sofa in his U.N. Plaza apartment. He is sitting on the arm of a sofa, unraveling a string of christmas tree lights. A large tree is stage left. **TRUMAN** wears slacks, a turtle-necked sweater and a windbreaker. His feet are in fleece-lined slippers, and on his head is an Irish tweed hat set at a rakish tilt.)*

TRUMAN. *(into the phone)* I do believe...it has something to do with frogs...yes.

*(Sound of service doorbell. **TRUMAN** rises.)*

Bells are ringing. Backdoor. Could it be the Three Magi? Don't go away...I'm coming, don't slam the door.

(He walks out to answer service door. We have a moment to take in the room which is the dining end of a large living space. The dining table is covered with packages and wrapping paper and Christmas decorations. This area also contains bookshelves and a sofa and chairs. The place is cozy and personal; the owner's ad hoc possessions, his very personality overcoming the decorator's hand. There is a great abundance of furniture, pictures, objects.)

Oh Lordy! I see it but I don't believe it!

*(**TRUMAN** returns, his hands filled with a pot of red poinsettias which he deposits on the floor and regards with dismay. He returns to the phone.)*

You can't conceive what just arrived. A veritable horse trough of unspeakable poinsettias... No, I do not know who from. I am going to dispose of the card sight unseen. It would shock and appall me to learn that somebody I like or even know would send me such a tacky thing. Poinsettias are the Bob Goulet of Botany.

Now. I need a little dirt fix. What is everybody up to?... Me? Oh precious, my life is being conducted on the highest possible plane. Don't let me even commence. Two glasses of wine, maximum. I swear...Why?... Because I am in New York to hold my head high and show the flag, not to roll in the gutter and gratify my enemies. So every evening I go out on my rounds and, my dear, I've been to seven parties in two days. Not bad for a social pariah...I carry a half-full glass of wine for hours to confound their spies! Hehehe...of course last night I came home desperately sober at three a.m. and gobbled up an entire box of chocolate truffles...then, of course, I had to go and take two tetracyclines so my face wouldn't break out!

(Laughs - the phone rings.)

Other line. Hang on... *(punches button)* Yee...essss? Oh, hi! I want to talk to you. Let me say goodbye to the divine Miss G. Hang on. *(punches button)* Sweetie, it's the gossip Avvocato. I'll have to call you back. These are desperate times, dear, and lawyers take precedence. But I adore you, you gorgeous thing. Don't you ever die! Hugs, kiss, kiss. *(Quickly switches lines, manner changes. He sits up. All business.)* Thanks for getting back so fast with the contract memos...Yes, I did. Down to the last wherefore and whereas. It looks pretty good to me... Well, a nonrefundable advance of one hundred and eighty seven thousand five for reprint rights? Not too shabby. I say let's grab it and run...Uh-huh.... Uh-huh ...yeesss, I am sitting down. Why?... *(As he listens, his eyes narrow.)* Oh yeah? I don't suppose Mr. Billy Redanty was careless enough to let you find out where he was calling you from?... Uh-huh...Well, if that pig-turd calls again, you tell him I've got my bone-cruncher out looking for him with a baseball bat, and it is my Christmas prayer that when he finds him, he will kill him. Okay? Will you just convey that message to Mr. Redanty?...And Avvocato dear, you know I'm serious. Rick's really lookin for Billy. And if he finds him, I'm gonna need a criminal lawyer. Now if you don't mind, I would like to elevate the tone of this conversation. What I wanted to tell you is I've decided to let Gerald Clarke have whatever he thinks he needs, so if he calls and asks for stuff from the files...Why not? All my life I've told things about myself that would make a baboon blush blue. I've been spilling the beans ever since I could talk. So my Boswell isn't exactly plowing virgin soil…Well… I'll, maybe a little discretion with the files. Hehehe. But I'm here to tell you, hon, letting down your hair with your biographer is very soothing. You can't imagine his tendresse and how he absolutely hangs on every word… *(listens a moment, then shrugs)* Oh, well…

(sings)

TRUMAN. *(cont.)* Don't worry, sugar. Like the man said, it's a long life, and "mostly untrue."

(roars with laughter) Listen. I'm going for drinks at Jan's, then we're meeting Ava Gardner and her crowd at Quo Vadis. Want to join us? Good for business, Avvocato. That outfit around Ava is very vivacious, if you know what I mean. They frequently find themselves in need of skilled courtroom advocates…Well, too bad then. And Listen. And I'm expecting that forty-five thousand from Columbia on time. Because Christmas is going to be very expensive this year. I'm giving stuff from Tiffany's and I'm getting poinsettias!

(With a big explosive laugh, he hangs up. Sits still for a moment, staring blankly. Then he rises purposefully and goes to stereo set, turns up volume. Armstrong is now in the middle of La Vie En Rose**.* **TRUMAN** *turns to Christmas tree and begins to string lights. Armstrong finishes* La Vie *and begins* Basin St. Blues. **TRUMAN** *listens, smiles faintly and moves easily into a quick little soft shoe step. He holds the pose a minute, goes to stereo and takes out the Armstrong tape.)*

I love ya, Louie, but we need something merry.

(He puts in another tape. It is the Supremes' Boy from Ipanema**. He nods, turns it fairly low, then he moves to pick up a small dictating machine, clicks it on, speaks into it.)*

---

*See Music Use Note on page 3.

For the ears of Gerald Clarke. Gary, know when I told you about my early encounter with Louis Armstrong?... Gary, I could just see you figuring, okay, you could write, "Truman claimed when he was four he danced on a riverboat where Louis Armstrong played. He claimed Armstrong called him a fine little dancer and took up a collection for him." *(drinks from his glass)* I could just see the clanking around in your head, Gary. But I did dance with Louis Armstrong, and I know where to find a corroborating witness. You're just gonna have to learn to trust me. I have lived an astonishing life. I've known everybody. *(sits cross-legged on hassock, settling in to tell the machine a story)* I bet I'm the only person in the world who knew Sirhan Sirhan and Robert Kennedy who also knew Lee Harvey Oswald and Jack Kennedy. The odds against that...one person knowing all four of those men...odds beyond reckoning, my dear. I met Oswald in Moscow just after he defected.

Out of five people killed in the Tate house the night Mr. Manson came to call, I knew four of the victims independently of each other. (Quite a coincidence.) I knew Garbo and Chaplin since my very first visit to Hollywood. I knew Marilyn Monroe well. I knew Martin Luther King and I knew Adlai Stevenson. As a matter of fact, we were staying in the same house when he died. When I heard I quickly ran in and chose one of his neckties. A very nice man. *(a beat)* Andy Warhol once confided me and me alone that he'd always wanted someone to call him "Daddy". So Gary, when I tell you I once tap danced on a riverboat with Louis Armstrong...know what I mean, Gary?

(Grins, flips off recorder. Looks out at audience. Stands, walks downstage, speaks directly to the audience.)

I've known everybody, And I've lived all over the world ...in this country I've lived in Louisiana, Alabama, Connecticut, Brooklyn, Mississippi, Manhattan, Long Island, Kansas, Palm Springs. And at a further remove, Moscow, Italy, France, Switzerland...I went to Staten

Island once. It was like Australia. *(gestures the room)* This is my apartment in the United Nations Plaza on New York's East River. I've had Johnny and Joanne Carson and Robert Kennedy for neighbors and we all have these fantastic views. *(gestures the expanse of windows)* We all look out on the United Nations. It's lovely to sit here with drinks and this phonograph on just at twilight, when all the lights in the city begin to go on. So stick around. *(begins to move around the space, pointing out a variety of objects)* What else can I tell you? I collect stuff...paperweights...*(picks one up, holds it for the audience to see)*

TRUMAN. *(cont.)* This one was given to me many years ago by Colette. Baccarat. It's now worth fifteen grand. *(puts paperweight down, gestures book cases)* Books, books, ever more books. A number of plaster cast...inappropriate Victoriana... *(happily)* I am the Decorator's Despair. Poor lady. Such good taste. However. Good taste is the death of art, you know. *(gestures entire room)*

Anyway, I collect things like a magpie. However, I don't love them much once I've got them. I have very little sense of possession. If I have learned anything, it is that you can't ever really own anything– *(laughs)* You're just sitting there waiting for me to say, "especially," Right? Wellllll, I guess we've all noticed how you can never, never own another person. But another person can own you. It's a very strange equation.

Like my hat? I wear hats a lot now... *(takes it off, shakes his head and runs fingers through his badly thinning hair)*

The receding locks of the aging poet. The Poet Laureate of the Lavatory Wall. *(beat)* That's what they're saying, anyway. At this particular moment in my life I stand accused of obscene treachery and betrayal because three months ago to sort of jolt myself out of a depression, I let *Esquire* publish a chapter from a novel I've been working on for twenty years. The novel's called

Answered Prayers. The title's from St. Teresa of Avila. She wrote, "More tears are shed over answered prayers than unanswered ones." St. Teresa was one sharp little cookie cutter.

Anyway, *Answered Prayers* is the book I've been in training for my whole life. It's going to be my *Vanity Fair,* my *Remembrance Of Things Past.* You know how they say everybody has one book in them? Well, I've written a lot of books, but basically I've always had this one book to justify...everything.

What's it about? *Answered Prayers* is about them. The Super Rich. As seen through the eyes of an outsider who for various reasons has privileged access. Hehehe, It's about sexual license and ethical squalor. Sexual license and ethical squalor.

(cheerfully) Camus once said, "My God, I've only written a tenth of what I know and they're already screaming." I know what he meant!

All this brouhaha over that one little chapter? Which was nothing really but a very truthful and may I say witty account of a bunch of silly people sitting in a restaurant dishing the dirt on each other. I used a couple of real names and certain attributes of some others... but my God, you'd think I killed the Lindbergh baby! What's the big deal! *(He takes out a clipping.)* Want to hear what Liz Smith wrote in *New York Magazine?* "Truman Capote in Hot Water: Society's sacred monsters are in a state of shock. Never have you heard such gnashing of teeth, such shouts of betrayal." As if I were Franklin Roosevelt...a traitor to my class. Which is hog-dash. I am not one of them. I am an artist. Artists belong to no class. And people like that who cozy up to artists do sat their own risk.

(A grim little smile. Laughs, suddenly eyeing the poinsettias, he puts his drink down. Goes to phone and dials, his call is answered immediately.)

TRUMAN. *(cont.)* Jimmy H., this is Mr. Capote. I 'm going to put a recently orphaned poinsettia plant out the back door for anyone who wants to give it a good home. Okay?

(He hangs up, picks up the plant, starts out of the room. He sings If Ever I Would Leave You.* *The phone rings. He hesitates, then continues out. On the third ring we hear* **TRUMAN***'s voice on the tape:)*

TRUMAN'S VOICE. Hellloo. I'm not in right now. When you hear the beep, just do yo' stuff.

(We then hear Truman's back door close, then the tape's beep. **TRUMAN** *re-enters the room as a young woman's voice comes over the phone.)*

VOICE. Mr. Capote, this is Betty, Mrs. White's secretary. Mrs. White had to go to the dentist and asked me to call you about a couple of inquiries. One from this ladies' literary society in Louisville, offering to almost double your fee. It's for the week of February seventh. That would set a precedent and Mrs. White said if you took this gig for that fee, she could maybe up your price on the whole circuit,...

*(***TRUMAN*** clicks on the phone.)*

TRUMAN. Oh, that's wonderful. Listen, hon, when Irene gets back in, ask her when Norman Mailer stabbed his wife, how much his fee went up? *(He hangs up. To audience:)* It's television. I used to be famous because I wrote books. Now I'm famous for being famous. Fame is only good for one thing...they'll cash your check in a small town.

So where was I? Oh yes. The Rich...and I don't count anyone as really rich who cannot quickly summon up fifty million in hard currency and I spent twenty years in the company of the big rich. I've flown everywhere in their planes– jets with queen-sized beds and marble loos and extensive video libraries of pornography. I've

---

*See Music Use Note on page 3.

eaten their wonderful fetal food, their little fresh-born vegetables...the baby lamb that has been ripped from its mother's womb...they eat well and take great care of their bodies. And they never hit you up for a loan. *(laughs)* Speaking of taking care of your body...

(He starts to jog easily in place.)

My idea of exercise is massage, with me being the massagee, not the masseur. Isn't it boring? But the Rich... most of them are pretty sad. Most of them would be totally lost without their money. That's why it means so much to them. Why they're so fixated on the subject.

(stops jogging, comes forward)

One time I was on the Agnelli yacht with Gianni and Marella and Princess Pignatelli, and about six other guests. Well, we were cruising on the Yugoslav coast. The Princess was just about to go to America. Every day, up and on the top deck, the princess was doing endless exercises. Stretching, bending, sunning, keeping herself slim and gilt. When she wasn't primping she was reading a book. It was a book in English. She read every word with her lips. It was slow going and I became fascinated as to the contents of this book that the gorgeous Luciana was reading with such forbidding intensity. So one day I sneaked over and I peeked at the cover. The title of it was, *The One Hundred Richest Americans*. A couple of days later we were steaming out of some little Jugland harbor where we'd taken on a lot of fresh vegetables and fruit. We all sat down to lunch and the steward served the first course which consisted of these rather exceptional melons. Marella tasted her melon and she said, "Oh, how absolutely divine. I could get drunk and disorderly on melons. Where did they come from?" Whereupon, the Princess perks up her ears and says, "The Mellons? The Mellons?–They come from Pittsburgh."

(Big laugh. He goes for another drink.)

TRUMAN. *(cont.)* Money, money, money! They're very nervous with you if they think you don't have any. That's why they hang together so desperately. It's not that they like each other...they don't. A yacht and five houses are what they have in common. And they get very bored with each other. So when they can, they try to take in amusing artists...If they were smart, they'd confine their patronage to the merely artistic. No billionaire ever got bit by Mario Buatta. *(takes a sip of his drink, walks back downstage, speaks familiarly)*

Any normal person with a normal sense of self-preservation would understand that all any artist has is his life and what he observes as he passes through his life. Any serious writer hanging out for years with the rich...You would have to be deluded to the point of derangement not to know that that writer was taking notes. My God, I even told them. Everybody knew I was writing this book. What did they think I was there for? The intellectual stimulation? The wit? The spiritual uplift? I'm the one who brought intellect and wit to the party. Yes, and the spiritual uplift, too, if anybody was buying. So. So. A few doors have been temporarily closed. Gloria Vanderbilt, the Paley's, the Whitneys, the Cowles, Lady Keith...I am being punished for having the bad taste to write humorously about a few a their crowd's less appetizing, what shall I say? Attitudes? And in a rage of sycophancy their hangers-on, their pilot-fish are violently vindictive. For instance, my own agent, Mr. Swifty Lazar...first time in fifteen years he didn't invite me to one of his big parties. Well, that ought to bring me to my senses! What they want is for me to grovel at their feet...maybe take a judicious little overdose and check in to Payne Whitney. Have my shrink call and say it's from a broken heart...Well, as my good friend Norman Mailer used to write, "fug' em." I am an artist and I am writing a masterpiece and they are wrong. In any event, I don't give a shit about any of them except the

Paleys and Slim Keith. Only those three. And I'm confident that in time Babe and Slim will come around. Very confident. *(talks to self)*

Maybe you're the kind of people that never talk to yourselves. Aloud, I mean. Personally, I've done it all my life. And I consider it healthy. You get a lot of stuff out of your system. I like to talk to myself and about myself. So there. I was born in New Orleans and named Truman Streckfuss Persons. Some years later I took my stepfather's name, Capote. When I was a child, I was called Buddy or Little T. Since I came to New York to work when I was seventeen, some good friends started to call me Tru. Which has a resonance I like. Tru. I've been a writer since I was eight years old. When I was eight I just started writing. Out of the blue, uninspired by any example. I'd never known anyone who wrote. I'd known very few who even read. Even my ambition to be a tap dancer was more acceptable to the people that I lived with than the idea of a writer in their midst. So write I did and write I do. *(a big smile)* Actually, I think I would have been good at anything I'd wanted to do. I'm very ept. I can ice-skate and ski. I can read upside down.

I can hit a tossed can with a .38 revolver. I have driven a Maserati at dawn on a flat, lonely Texas road at one hundred and seventy miles an hour. I can cook, oh can I cook and I can dance. I mean tap dance. *(does a time step)*

Bet you didn't expect that. I can type sixty words a minute and I'm an alcoholic. It's a chemical addiction not a psychological one...I can scarcely think of a writer who's not a heavy drinker. One or two. Arthur Miller, of course. Well, but there aren't many who don't have the problem. Writing is hard and you get depressed and every few years I slide into one of those things and it's not at all pleasant and I try to take it in stride.

TRUMAN. *(cont.)* And whenever I feel things are getting out of control I check myself into a hospital to get the poisons wiped out. I don't believe these should be any opprobrium whatsoever attached to this. It's just common sense. I've been in Silver Hill and Riggs, and a lovely place out in Minnesota. Even a couple of emergency rooms. *(grins)* I wish I had a bit more confidence in psychiatry. I feel a bit like Tennessee Williams who once confided in me that he was going to quit his analysis. "Truman," he said, "That man is tryin' to interfere in my private life!"

(Laughs. Very cheerfully now.)

Also. They're always so excessively concerned with homosexuality. Well, I've never had any problem with being a homosexual. I was always right out there.

I have always been an object of desire. Yes I was. When I was in school, I was amusing and I was pretty. Very popular. Everybody wanted to go to bed with me. From the headmaster on down. God, I'm practically the number one person around who has had everybody who everybody else said was straight about women. I think most people don't have any idea what their sexual identity is. I've always said that if you decide you want somebody...I don't care who they are...if you really want them and you concentrate exclusively, you will probably get that person. That has been my experience. Very few people can resist when somebody really, really wants them. When somebody focuses totally on them. One, it's so flattering and two, if it goes on long enough it just wears them down. *(laughs)* Energy helps too.

I am very energetic when the occasion arises. Hehehe. The main thing about me is that I am not like anybody else. Most homosexuals are very ordinary people, but not me. There is nothing ordinary about me. I was always a sort of two-headed calf. As a child I was aware of this at a very early age. For openers, I am distinctly curious-looking, wouldn't you agree? And everybody's always making allusions to this weird little voice Capote has, and describing me as "delicate"? I'm about as delicate as a pit bull. In actual fact I have a sturdy peasant frame, I'm a good athlete. An excellent swimmer and diver. What else? I'm responsible with money and a good businessman. My age? Oh, I never tell my age. I'm fifty-one. *(laughs)*

(long beat)

And for fifty one years...ever since I can remember, I've lived with this feeling of dread, the belief that any minute something terrible is going to happen. Like you're on the drop of the gallows. Oh, I mean, I've literally stood and watched people on the drop of the gallows, held their hand, a minute before, then watched them drop and their heads jerk back and their feet dance...that moment before it's going to happen, I believe I know how that moment feels.

When I researched *In Cold Blood* I interviewed literally hundreds of convicted murderers. Many of them on Death Row. Once in Hong Kong, I was walking through the market and saw all these little dogs in bamboo cages. The cages were stacked on top of each other, and the little dogs were stuffed inside; very passive, not yapping. Nothing. It was very hot. I couldn't imagine what in the world they were there for, so I asked the Chinese girl who was with me. "Oh," she said, "They're for sale. They're waiting to be eaten. Soup is made of those little dogs."

That was many years ago. But the first time I saw Death Row in one of our prisons, all I could think of was those little dogs. I identify with those little dogs. And with those convicted killers. *In Cold Blood*, how much it took out of me.

(He moves to table, picks up a wrapped package, attaches a tag to it. He smiles, pleased. This contains a collection of swatches.)

TRUMAN. *(cont.)* It's fabric swatches for my editor, Joe Fox. I'm giving him a custom made three-piece suit from Dunhill's. It'll change his life.

(smiles knowingly at audience) Have you ever fantasized about killing somebody? You haven't? No? Cross your heart? Well, I still don't believe you. Everybody at one time or another has wanted to kill someone. As for me, if desire had ever been transformed into action, I'd be right up there with Jack the Ripper. Plotting murder is somewhat relaxing but not relaxing enough. I am seldom able to sleep without chemical aid. I feel as if I've never spent a tranquil moment in my life.

(He begins to wrap another box.)

It is reasonable to assume that this monstrous anxiety of mine comes from being an unwanted child. My parents were separated soon after I was born. My mother quickly realized what a big mistake she'd made. She was very pretty and other men entered her life, and she left me with her three maiden sisters and unmarried brother in Monroeville, Alabama, population one thousand three hundred and a few odd souls. I can remember standing in the street and watching her drive off…getting smaller and smaller and smaller…

(long beat)

The family wasn't unkind to me. In a way it was very hard on them, because they definitely thought something was wrong with me.

(He takes a pill from his sweater pocket. He pops it dry. He moves toward the tree begins to add ornaments to its branches.)

I'm very ambivalent about Christmas. I want it to be magic—warm and lavish with all your friends like a family. Which sets up terrible anxiety because I don't have a very good history with Christmases. And that's true with most alcoholics, you know.

"Things happen."

(shrugs) This year is notable for the painful number of absent friends. I'm not talking about that crowd...I mean like Jack...I asked him not to go to Switzerland this year, but to stay and see me through this Christmas, but as usual he escaped. Oh, you don't know Jack Dunphy and I have been together almost thirty years...lovers for three and best friends and closest companions ever since. We've been through it all together. Together, but not necessarily under the same roof, or, during my more trying periods, on the same continent. *(indicates Christmas tree)* Who am I doing this for? *(laughs)* I had thought that this Christmas... with most of the city's celebrants behaving as if I were spreading cholera...maybe he'd stick around and offer a little support.

And on my split with Billy...my split with Billy...well from the beginning Jack always said Billy was a user. *(beat)* Jack doesn't know. I know what Billy is. And more important what he isn't. "Billy Middleclass," he calls himself. *(a wry grin)* Billy denies he's homosexual. But I first picked him up in a gay bathhouse. Mr. Redanty is a sadist, an, alcoholic, a big spender of other people's money...he tried to interfere in my work. He's a braggart and a liar and a social embarrassment and a thief. He's also an embezzler. Aside from the twenty thousand he recently appropriated from me, he has also stolen six spiral notebooks containing fifteen years work on *Answered Prayers*. Which is the major reason I am having trouble finishing it. So you can see why I sincerely hope my friend with the baseball bat gets a shot at him.

(Averts his gaze, shrugs, feels in his pocket. Takes out a joint, puts it in his mouth, and lights up, takes a deep drag. Holds it for a moment before exhaling.)

However...if Billy stopped drinking...*(takes another drag, lets it out)*

TRUMAN. *(cont.)* If I stopped drinking…and everything was straight…if I really can't, get him out of my system, maybe we could still have a life together.

(beat, a small smile)

Absent Friends.

(He goes to the sofa).

Oh go ahead. Do it.

(A look of determination on his face, he picks up phone and dials. The ring is promptly answered.)

Hello, I want to send a telegram…This is 756-1076. Yes, of course it is. That's my number. I want to send a telegram to Mr. and Mrs. William Paley at…no, make that just to Mrs. Paley. The address is Indian Hill Rd., Brookville, Long Island. I don't know the zip. The message is, "I am so sad and lonely for you, and it is positively unchristian that you should remain so unforgiving to a poor sinner over the hols"…Hols. Short for holidays. Now where was I?…Right. Uh, "…over the hols."

(beat)

"I love you and I miss you. And that's the solemn truth, Babe." Signed Tru. No I don't want you to read all that back, my God. *(beat)* Signed Tru. T…R…U.

(hangs up, sits there for a moment, then grimaces)

So? In for a penny, in for a pound.

(Dials again, as hs waits for his call to be answered, he picks up the joint. It has gone out. He switches on phone amplifier and gets up to find a match to re-light the joint.)

(We hear the operators voice.)

OPERATOR. Hello, this is Western Union. May I help you?

TRUMAN. Hello, I am calling 756-1076 and I want it charged to that number. The message is for Lady Nancy Keith…

OPERATOR. Would you spell that first name please.

TRUMAN. *(smiles)* L-A-D-Y, Lady. Lady Nancy Keith. K-E-I-T-H. The address is 100 Merryall Road, New Milford, Connecticut, 06776. The message is, "Merry Christmas, Big Mama. I've decided to forgive you. Love, Tru...T-R-U." Would you read that back please?

OPERATOR. It goes to Lady, L-A-D-Y Nancy Keith, K-E-I-T-H, 100 Merryall Road, New Milford, Connecticut, 06776. The message is "Merry Christmas, Big Mama. I've decided to forgive you."

(TRUMAN grins, pleased with himself)

Signed Tru. T-R-U. Is that all?

TRUMAN. *(wryly)* That's actually quite a lot, sugar.

OPERATOR. Excuse me for asking, but are you Truman Capote?

(TRUMAN walks back to phone, sits down.)

TRUMAN. *(parodies own voice)* Why aren't you something, you clever thing, however did you guess?

OPERATOR. She's the one they call "Slim", isn't she? Slim Keith?

TRUMAN. *(delighted with this exchange)* Welllll, she once was. Slim, that is.

OPERATOR. Well, I think she's acting ridiculous. I just want to say I think they all are. A bunch of real assholes. They ought to be honored you wrote about them. I read *Breakfast at Tiffany's* and *In Cold Blood*, and you're a wonderful writer.

TRUMAN. Thank you from the bottom of my heart. What's your name, hon?

OPERATOR. Judy, Judy Kornbleu.

TRUMAN. Well, Judy, I want to wish you a Glorious Christmas.

OPERATOR. You too, Mr. Capote.

TRUMAN. Call me Tru.

OPERATOR. Hey, how about that! Well, a glorious Christmas to you, Tru.

(**TRUMAN** *laughs and hangs up phone, flicks off audio button.*)

TRUMAN. Sometimes there's God. The truth is I've been fighting off the worst case of the mean reds I've maybe ever had in my life. And that's saying a lot. I wake up some of these mornings and I feel like I've been snake bit. And I know what I'm talking about. When I was eight years old I was bitten by a cottonmouth water moccasin. The scariest part was that they killed a bunch of chickens, and ripped them open. The hot chicken flesh was supposed to draw out the poison and I guess it did, because the chicken meat turned green and I didn't. But I sure enough felt as if I had been snake bit. My God. I didn't bomb Pearl Harbor! I didn't kill the Kennedys.

(*Makes a visible effort to relax. Goes to mix himself another drink.*)

(*beat*)

I'm not an unkind person. I'm not judgmental, I'm a generous and caring fried, and no matter what they say, a loyal one. I'm not a cheat. I'm very very honest. (*shakes his head*)

Lord. Even as a child. Well, once. I stepped over the line once. I committed one serious crime. When I was eight. What I did…my crime was I stole my grandmother's necklace. I stole it to pay Mrs. Ferguson that's why. Mrs. Ferguson was a fancy laundress, probably the only white laundress in New Orleans. She was said to have magical powers. It was said, and believed by many… certainly by me…that she could tame errant husbands, restore lost hair, recoup squandered fortunes. In short, she was a witch who could make wishes come true.

(*sips his drink, moves restlessly around the room, sucks hungrily on the marijuana*)

I had a secret wish, something I was afraid to tell anybody. Anybody. Except Mrs. Ferguson. I wanted to tell my secret to Mrs. Ferguson. I felt I had to.

(He sits on the downstage bench.)

But how could I pay? What could I give her? Wellll... What I could give her it turned out, was my grandmother's necklace. It was a dazzling yellow stone. When Mrs. Ferguson first saw the necklace, her ignorant moon eyes glowed, they truly glowed. That is a fact. The deal she offered me was my wish for my grandmother's necklace. I knew if I were caught, I'd never be forgiven.

(TRUMAN's head ducks in remembered shame.)

But I had to have it. I stole it and I ran.

(TRUMAN's head comes up slowly as the apartment lights dim. His eyes focus somewhere on his childhood. He speaks in a small and timorous voice.)

TRUMAN. Mrs. Ferguson?

(The lights dim even further. We hear Mrs. Ferguson's voice surrounding TRUMAN.)

MRS. FERGUSON'S VOICE. Where is it, Boy?

TRUMAN. *(whispering)* Here. In my pocket.

(He holds out his hand.)

MRS. FERGUSON'S VOICE. Well? Am I expected to guess? Am I supposed to tell you why you're here? What is it you want? Well?

TRUMAN. I...What...I like...I like to tap dance. *(speaking quickly, not lying but not telling her the real truth)* I want to be a tap dancer. I want to run away. I want to go to Hollywood and be in the movies.

MRS. FERGUSON'S VOICE. Well, you sure are pretty enough to be in picture shows. Prettier than any boy ought to be.

TRUMAN. *(shouts)* Yes! Yes! That's it! That's it! I don't want to be a boy! I want to be a girl! That's my wish!

(The woman begins to laugh.)

Please, please Mrs. Ferguson. I'm very worried...Don't laugh!

MRS. FERGUSON'S VOICE. Ain't you somthin'...Ain't you jest some kind of little he-she little twoheaded calf of a young 'un! No wonder your mama took off and all them others wantin to get shed of you!

TRUMAN. You shut up! Shut up! Shut up!

(The phone rings. The lights come up slightly; **TRUMAN** *stands transfixed. When the phone has rung three times, we hear his voice on the answering machine.)*

TRUMAN'S VOICE. Helloooo. I'm not in right now. When you hear the beep, just do yo' stuff.

WOMAN'S VOICE. Tru? Where you? We're all just sitting here waiting for you...*(in the background, party sounds)* There's nothing to eat and people are getting smashed. If you don't call back or show up in fifteen minutes, we're going on to Quo Vadis and...Tru, are you there? We're going to Quo Vadis in fifteen minutes, OK? Are you there?

(As she has spoken, the lights have gone up full and **TRUMAN***, emerging from his memory of Mrs. Ferguson, moves to the phone, picks it up.)*

TRUMAN. Jan. I'm sorry...I've been working and just lost track of the time. All I've got to do is find the appropriate chapeau to put the spell on Miss Ava. I'll meet you all at the restaurant. And Sugar...know what you are?...What you are is an absolutely perfect person. I'll see you all shortly, bye.

(He hangs up, moves to pick up the remains of his drink, kills it. He walks to the stereo to punch tape on. What begins to play is the Supremes' Santa Claus is Comin' to Town*. still distracted,* **TRUMAN** *stands a moment until the insistent rhythm gets to him. Then he gives himself to it, throws off his black memories and tap dances off.)*

END OF ACT I

---

*See Music Use Note on page 3.

ACT II

(Before the curtain goes up we hear a chorus of Ella Fitzgerald's At Long Last Love*. It is late the next afternoon. Christmas Eve. The tree is now fully decorated. The lights are not on. But the tree is fulsomely dressed with an abundance of presents underneath. The long table is clear of clutter with a beautiful arrangement of flowers on it. There are other flowers scattered about the room which looks orderly and festive. As in the first act, it is once again late afternoon.)*

*(***TRUMAN** *is wearing slacks and a T-shirt over which is wrapped a short silk kimono. He is on the phone. On the table beside him is a tray with a thermos of coffee and a cup and saucer. It is clear that he is suffering a severe hangover.)*

TRUMAN. It's not at all complicated and no, I don't want to wait till Mr. Rudy gets back…Yes, of course I know it's Christmas Eve. That's why I'm giving you an order for thousands of dollars worth of flowers. Well, you'll just have to be reasonable. What's your name? …"Jesus?" how apropos. Well, Jesus, honey, you just look in the file under Capote and you'll find two lists of names and addresses. Many names. One list is marked "A" and one list is marked "B." The "A" list is to get narcissus and the "B" list is to get white orchid plants. Isn't that simple? …Narcissi for A, Orchids for B …Oh, Rudy. Where in the world have you been? Hi! I just gave the order to Jesus. Flats of narcissi for…just like last year, yes…Well, I know it's Christmas Eve, yessss, and I know it's a very long list, but I just got in from Russia an

---

*See Music Use Note on page 3.

hour ago, hon, and...Oh, Rudy, I know you can do it if you just make some calls. I'm not asking for arrangements! Now don't sob, Rudy. It 's the season to be jolly. Like it or not...Just do the best you can, okay? Please Jingle Bell? *(He hangs up. Holds his throbbing temples.)* I am not a good person.

(The phone rings.)

TRUMAN. *(cont.)* Christ!

*(**TRUMAN** flinches, picks it up quickly.)*

Whoever you are, please speak softly...yes, yes, I can hear you...Oh Jack! Hi! Hi, is it absolutely perfect there? Are you wallowing in Swiss Perfection?...Wellll, not exactly... Wellll. I meant to call you. I think I might actually have tried. But I couldn't swear...Nothing. nothing. Last night I made the mistake of trying to keep up with Miss Ava Gardner. Miss Gardner is muy macho. In her wake I sort of fell into the drink, so to speak ...now don't fuss. I'm okay. We went discoing and I think I just danced it out of my system. Disco...Disco. You know... Aerobics. Very good for you. So except for these castanets doing their thing inside my cranium, I'm actually okay. I slept last night. And I'm up and bustling and tending to business today. It is Christmas Eve. You know...of course I've got the tree up. Of course I decorated it myself...it looks very pretty. Well. I'm going to Jan's with some very nice people. Among whom I wish I could number you...No...I'm all right. Really, I am...And I am not going to drink any more... No. I have not disgraced myself...I know because I know. I may not remember every single moment, but I remember most of it. Just discoing and laughing it up and seeing a few friends... Lord. Jack, I don't remember who all. It's Christmas. The city's swarming...Well, I wish so too. I really do. *(a long beat)* Now, don't fret. I'm perfectly fine. And Jan's been very, very supportive. Also C.Z. Very staunch...I'll call you tomorrow. After I open your present...Bye now. I'm glad you called. Bye bye.

(He hangs up. Turns and stares at the Christmas tree.)

The guy who does the night run on my service elevator claims he does twenty-four miles a night up and down. So I have him a travel clock from Tiffany. I gave it to him for decorating that shitty old tree.

(buzzer sounds)

Tributes, tributes…more tributes.

(A picture is delivered.)

A plain brown wrapper. Something naughty? I hope—

(unwraps picture—shows to audience)

My glory days. The way we were. *(He reads card.)* "Dear old Tru-Cat. As you might have heard I an moving to Morocco with Himself who objects violently to this reminder of Les Temps Perdu. So rather than consign it to auction I thought it should go to you. Merry Christmas and Love. Davey."

(He looks at the picture.)

Les Temps Perdu indeed. *(snaps folding fan, grins)* You all disco? You know Studio 54? I love it. It's sooo democratic. Boys with girls, boys with boys, girls with girls, blacks and whites. Capitalists and Marxists…All one big mix. What I really like is to sit in the deejay's booth. Sometimes when I'm up there I think about all the dead people who would have loved it. Toulouse-Lautrec and Cleopatra. It's so glamorous. Cole Porter would have loved it.

(He feels in his pocket. Comes up with a pill that he pops. Sighs. A moment of silence.)

Oh shit. You know what I'd really like? I'd like to get dressed up and go to lunch with Babe and tell her everything that was going on at Studio 54. It's so stupid this thing that's happened with *Answered Prayers*. Stupid and ridiculous and childish. I didn't do anything. I'd never deliberately consciously do anything to hurt Babe. She used to say to me, "There's only one person in the world who could hurt me. Bill can't hurt me or my sisters, but you could really hurt me." And apparently I did. Bizarre and ridiculous as that seems. And because I love her, she is hurting me too…out of loyalty to a husband who is so disloyal to her. My God. I didn't name Bill, like I did some of the people in the story. I did not describe him. His attitude maybe…but that attitude is no singular to Bill Palev. The world is full of rich shits. When Babe first read the story, she didn't recognize him. It was other people trouble… *(shrugs angrily)* People can only tolerate so much success. It's as simple as that. Well. they can kiss my serene ass on my couch of many colors, because except for Babe I couldn't care less. Babe and Slim.

Slim will come around. Want to bet? If she doesn't make a gesture before February first. I'll nail her on Valentine's Day. I'm her closest friend, and she needs me. The truth is, I'm very good news for all those women. Those beautiful, intelligent, privileged, lonely women. They are absolutely crazy about me, and that's a fact. Why? Because damn it, I like them. I pay attention to them. I listen. I understand their problems. I make them laugh. I tell them how to dress, what makeup to wear, what to read and who to love. When they're miserable, I tuck them into bed and tell them bedtime stories…What they like best is something horrendous about someone impeccable.

(beat)

TRUMAN. *(cont.)* Don't we all.

(beat)

Ava Gardner. Ava's fun. After Christmas we're going to England together to a fat farm. And for a change, I'm the one getting the advice. She said, "Honey, stop worrying about your mental health. Do a little something for yourself. Lose a few pounds and get a face lift. Give yourself a chance at an interesting future." She's a very down to earth, practical, Southern girl. And I'm going to follow her counsel. *(beat)* Cicero said life is a moderately good play with a badly written third act.

(laughs) Well, I'm going to try to at least put some good scenes and a few laughs into my third act. Did you know that homosexuals are the employees of choice in the royal households? Princess Margaret validated that information for me. It's completely understandable. The boys are unburdened by families, of course, and they cheerfully work long hours for short pay. Anyway I have this friend who used to work in Buckingham Palace. He said that one day about five-thirty he and a couple of other staff members were having a well-deserved drink when the phone rang. My friend answered it and it was the Queen Mum who was visiting. She said, "Is that you, Nigel?" He said, "Yes Ma'am, it is," and before he could go on she said, "Well, I don't know what you young queens are doing down there, but this old queen up here needs a drink." *(smiles)* Of course I believe it.

(The phone rings, he answers.)

Yesssssss?...Carole! You Doll! Merry Christmas!...Oh Lovey, I know you're not angry. I adore you, too...and don't worry that Gloria will find out you called. My lips are sealed. Of course my old Underwood can be very indiscreet, Hehehe...So, sugar pie, are you ready for Christmas? Have you spent oodles and oodles of Walter's money?...Good girl. Well, darling, you're the brightest and the best and I worship you and you are angelic to call...I'll see you in 1976. You're going to be astonished at the new me. I am going to trim down the tum and lift high the face...I am. There's going to be a brand new Tru. No booze and no Billy! I swear! Or any other evil companions. I am going to get healthy and finish the book...You know what I say now when somebody asks me if they're in it? Not yet. Well, like we say at Forest Lawn, not yet, but I've reserved a plot for you, we'll fit YOU all in. Hehehe...Okay, I will. I mean it. I'll call you on New Years Eve. Merry Christmas, Precious. Merry Christmas. You're the only one who called. Keep your chin up – Jingle Bell.

(hangs up)

TRUMAN. *(cont.)* Who the hell was that? Carol Matthau. Carol and Gloria Vanderbilt and Oona O'Neill Chaplin were teen-age pals, and in a kind of loony show of solidarity all three of those beautiful and gifted young women married dirty old men. Bizarre. *(laughs)* Carole's second husband is Walter Matthau and they live in California. I mean live there. All the time. It's a scientific fact that for every year you stay in California you lose two points off your I.Q. It's redundant to die in L.A. But old people love it. They close their eyes, and the wind whispering through the winter flowers says sleep, the sea says sleep…

(beat)

Well, I am definitely not ready to "sleep". In the deeper sense.

(And his eyes move longingly towards the bar, but he turns away, begins to move restlessly around the room, picking up an object, putting it down, straightening a picture. Suddenly stops, remembers something.)

Oh God. Where did I put it.

(He goes to the next room, gets a package, brings it back into living room, begins to unwrap it.)

Thank God! This is from a girl who occasionally does research for me. She always gives me a big bag of what used to be penny candy. *(begins to pick and choose)* Num. Num. Chockie kisses …Mal-teasers.

(pops the mal-teaser into his mouth and unwraps a chocolate kiss)

All-day suckers…Oh yum! Mary Janes! Remember? Molasses taffy and peanut butter! Little T's favorite…

(Pops another Mal-Teaser. Sticks three Mary Janes and an all-day sucker into his pocket.)

I won't eat the Mary Janes while I'm trying to talk.

(Satisfied, he now shoves a hassock downstage and sits down, facing the audience.)

I'm sorry not to pass it around. I must ask you to regard this stuff as medicinal. Which it is. For a metabolic problem. When somebody accustomed to a certain amount of alcohol every day doesn't get those carbohydrates, why then the body just sets up this demand. So I apologize.

(He unwraps the all-day sucker that he had pocketed earlier. He puts it in his mouth, sucks it gratefully, then smiles.)

Whenever she had an extra penny, Sook would buy me a grape all-day sucker. Sook was my mother's oldest sister...and yet the youngest. A lot of people thought she was retarded and the family treated her accordingly, accused her of being "funny," but she was just dreadfully shy. And innocent. *(goes to bookcase)* Actually I've been quoting from a book I wrote about Sook and me. *A Christmas Memory. (sits and begins to read)*

Sookie and I were like forgotten people. Sook by her brothers and sisters and me by my parents... We only identified with people outside the boundaries of our little town. I was extremely jealous of all the children whose names or pictures were in the newspaper. Shirley Temple, Bobby Breen, Jackie Cooper, everybody. Sook identified with people in the Bible. I am seven, she is sixty something and we are best friends.

Other people inhabit the house, relatives; and though they have power over us, and frequently make us cry, we were not, on the whole, too much aware of them. Sook and I took Christmas very seriously. Our biggest Christmas project was making fruit cakes. Who were they for?

People who struck our fancy...The year that I was seven I remember we made a cake for Abner Packer... the driver of the six o'clock bus from Mobile, who always exchanged waves with us every day as he passed in a dust-covered whoosh. And the knife grinder. And President Roosevelt.

TRUMAN. *(cont.)* All that year that I was seven, there was this little bit of whiskey left over from the fruit cake, so Sook and I, and Queenie...Queenie was our tough little rat terrier who did me one better by surviving snake bites –and anyway, Sook and Queenie and I drank that leftover whiskey and got drunk and caused a scandal.

Enter the relatives.

(reads again)

"Whiskey on his breath!"

"A child of seven?!"

"Remember Cousin Kate? Uncle Charlie?"

"Scandal! Humiliation! Kneel, pray!"

"Beg the Lord!"

In my seven year-old opinion the effects of the whiskey on me were lovely. The grown ups were stupid and mean. *(goes upstage to sofa, sits)*

After that Christmas everything changed. Because the next year my mother married Mr. Capote and, "those Who Know Best decide that I belong in military school." *(reading)* And so followed a miserable succession of bugle-blowing prisons, grim reveille-ridden summer camps. And finally... after my mother had given up getting a new baby by Mr. Capote, she sent for me. I have a new home, too. But it doesn't count. Home is where my friend is...and there...I never go...

(gets up, places book on coffee table)

So. Another New York Christmas.

Christmas in New York might work for O. Henry or Frank Capra, but it tends to go...askew for me. Things happen. *(a thought, grins)* The things we remember. Hehehe.

One Christmas...I was very young and living in this Greenwich Village walkup. It was Christmas Eve and there was a party I was sort of invited to, but it wouldn't start till late...after ten...I was alone in my apartment waiting for the time to pass…a little depressed. So I decided to open one of my presents. The one that caught my eye was a box from Bonwit Teller which made me hope that it was something nice. It was from a very naughty friend, and I feared it was a joke, but I hoped for something nice.

So I opened it. Well. What was in that box from Bonwit Teller was a girl's nightgown. A pink shortie with lots of ruffles.

(beat)

A fairly expensive joke, because the gown was really very pretty. Soooo… I put it on. Actually, I looked rather sweet. My spirits lifted. I was still at least an hour and a half til time to go to the party, so I just sort of drifted around the apartment straightening things up, taking out the trash…

(long beat)

…and got locked out in the hall. Barefooted in the new nightie. It was cold, six above zero, and I figured I couldn't afford to stand on my dignity, so I rang my neighbor's door bell. Both neighbors. No response. So I ran upstairs and tried the three apartments up there. Nothing. Nobody home. Frantic, I now decided to risk trying the owner's apartment on the ground floor. Welllll, in that whole shitty old brownstone there was not a living soul at home but me. It was Christmas Eve and clearly everybody in the world but me was out at a universal party. By now I was getting a little hysterical, not to say freezing, and I realized that I could huddle in that icy hallway for hours before any of the world's celebrants might finally wander home. So I decided there is nothing for it but to make a mad dash to the drugstore on the other end of my block. Which I did…running through the snow like little Eva with the hounds snapping at her ass! Praying that the drugstore would still be open. Well, it was and in I tumbled. There was nobody in the store but this old man behind the prescription counter. He took one look and yelled,

TRUMAN. *(cont.)* "What the hell is this?" And I explained my predicament, said I would have to have a nickel to use the phone to call somebody to come and help me and…

And he screamed! "Get out of here, you disgusting little fag! Get out of this store!"

Well, it wasn't going to do me any good to get haughty, because I had to have that nickel. So just as nice as pie I said how sorry I was, but I couldn't get out of his store until I got a nickel and called for help, and the quicker I got the nickel, the quicker somebody would come and remove me.

We stood there staring at each other for a very long minute, then he smacks the cash register and takes out a nickel and slams it down on the counter. "And after you make that call, you get inside…the phone booth! You hear me?"

Talk about no room at the inn! Anyway, I went to the phone booth and called a woman I knew, an editor, very kind, with a family, who I knew would be home. And in no time at all she arrived with a car and a coat which she started to bundle me into, but first I said, "Wait a second…I need a nickel." So she gave me one and I went over to the counter. The old man's face was still red with fury, but I smiled sweetly and put the nickel down on the counter. Then I took two steps back and said:

*(**TRUMAN** mimes a small girl pulling her dress up over her head. Giving the druggist a consummate flash.)*

"…And Merry Christmas to you, too!"

Baboomba.

(goes to candy, unwraps and eats a chocolate kiss)

The things we remember. Everybody tells me sugar's a killer no matter how you take it. It makes some people violent. But it calms me. Which I need. Because it is very important for me not to drink just now. Because I very much need to keep my wits about me.

My mother killed herself at Christmas. Christmas of 1953. I was in Italy when I got the news. She killed herself at 1066 Park Avenue. Which was, in its way, a success story. She was born in Monroeville Alabama, but she got out and she got a well-to-do husband... whom she loved and she died, regardless of how, on Park Avenue. My contacts with Grace Kelly and Princess Margaret were so important to her. She was beautiful and intelligent, but she didn't want to live. She had many reasons...at least she thought she did. So one night she got all dressed up and gave a dinner party. Everybody said she looked lovely. But after the party, before she went to bed, she took thirty Seconals and she never woke up.

(beat, a faint smile)

...All the people I've known who've killed themselves. Or really and truly tried... *(shrugs)* Marilyn, my mother, Monty Clift, Babe tried twice. I'm sorry life often turns out to be so fucking rotten. Look, anybody in their right mind thinks about suicide.

(beat)

I've always been almost overly aware of the precipice we walk along, the ridge on one side, the abyss on the other. But I'd never kill myself. Psychiatrists say that almost all suicides are the result of a terrible anger that a person turns against himself when he can't confront the person who has hurt him. Not me. Anyone who had worked me into that kind of state would find himself looking down the barrel of a shotgun! *(chuckles, then catches himself)*

What am I laughing about? *(beat)* The murderer's little laugh of social embarrassment. *(shrugs)* Well, there you are.

(a long beat)

Writing a truthful book...or story...there's always a touch of murder in it. I found that out when I was eight years old. Did I tell you I published my first story when I was eight?

TRUMAN. *(cont.)* There was this contest for children in the Mobile Register. I wrote a story called "Mrs. Busybody." My story was not along the customary lines of What-I-Did-On-My-Vacation. It was a sort of *Roman à clef*... about people I knew or knew about in Monroeville. About a very fat woman, very fat, who sat on her porch all day long and tried to murder her own child; a town bachelor who hated all women, even female dogs, and I forget who the others were. But whoever they were, they were real. Anyway, Well, "Mrs. Busybody" was supposed to come out in three separate installments, but when the first section was printed and everybody in Monroeville read it, the town went crazy, and that was that. Nobody ever saw the other two installments. After that, people stopped telling me things...some even stopped talking to me. And not long after that I began to dream. I've been having the same sad dream for over forty years. I'm eight years old and I'm walking down a dusty street in Monroeville, Alabama.

And when people see me coming they turn their backs and refuse to talk to me, because I've written about them.

That's all there is to the dream. Nothing so terrible. But I always wake up weeping. "...And our end is consequent on our beginning." So. *(smiles)* The main thing that history teaches us is history teaches us nothing. Right? Right.

What I keep thinking– what I keep thinking is that if I could just finish the book...or finally really dump Billy Redanty, or when I look beautiful again, everything will be all right. When I look beautiful again. It's so stupid. The drinking is stupid.

(beat)

The kids at Studio 54 gave me a little cocaine last night. Unfortunately, I had a few drinks so I didn't get the pure effect. They say I should take coke to help me stay off alcohol. Alcohol is such a fucking depressant. And who needs that?

(gets up–moves upstage)

You know how I said I would never commit suicide? Well, I don't think I would, but then I keep asking doctors for prescriptions for Tuinals, and they keep giving them to me. Listen. I've saved up enough Tuinals to stage my own Jonestown massacre.

Because you're never safe 'till they dial Frank Campbell. *(looks at pastel)* The way we were.

(Smashes pastel. Laughs.)

But - like the man said, "tis the season to be jolly" - - like it or not.

(goes to record player, changes tape. Plays Louis Armstrong's Sunny Side of the Street*, dances)*

Every move's a picture. *(He goes to sofa, plops down, sighs deeply.)* Boy, oh boy, oh boy, am I thirsty. Yes. Am I going to fix myself a drink? No. It's Christmas eve and you've got to give it all you've got.

(He picks up copy of A Christmas Memory.*)*

They made a lovely television show of this. Geraldine Page played Sook. *(pats book lovingly)* My beautiful Christmas memory.

(beat)

Speaking of memories, did you ever wonder what would go through your head if you were drowning?

(He gets up, comes downstage center.)

I have. Like home movies. *(His eyes focus on a spot above the heads of the audience.)* It's a hot Alabama day in…1932, so I must be eight…and I am in a vegetable garden humming with bees and heat waves, and I am picking turnips and slushy scarlet tomatoes. Then I am running through a pine and honeysuckle woods toward a deep cool creek where I bathe and wash the turnips, the tomatoes. Bird-music, leaf-light, the taste

---

*See Music Use Note on page 3.

of raw turnip on my tongue...pleasures everlasting, hallelujah. Not far away a snake, a cottonmouth moccasin, writhes, ripples across the water. I am not afraid of it.

(His gaze shifts to a different scene.)

TRUMAN. *(cont.)* Standing at the window of a pension on a Mediterranean island, watching the afternoon passenger boat arrive from the mainland. Suddenly, there on the wharf carrying a suitcase is someone I know, know very well. Someone who had said goodbye. Someone who has apparently had a change of mind. So. Is it the real turtle soup? Or only the mock? Or is it at long last love?

(He turns away from that memory, frowns.)

Now...a young man, with black cowlicked hair. He is wearing...a leather harness that keeps his arms strapped to his sides. He is trembling, speaking to me, smiling, but all I can hear is the roar of blood in my ears. Twenty minutes later he is dead, hanging from the end of a rope.

(A beat. A shrugging off. Finally, a small smile.)

Now...oh, now the mental slides are moving faster and faster...I am nursing to life a bulldog puppy ill to death with distemper. And she lives. Picking apples on an autumn afternoon. A face, close by. Is it the Taj Mahal I see? Or merely Asbury Park? Or is it at long last love. *(laughs shortly)*

It wasn't. God no, was it ever not!

It's 1966. My beautiful black and white ball at the Plaza Hotel. It cost me seventy five thousand. Worth every penny of it. Four hundred of my truest friends are there. The press called it the party of the decade. Betty Bacall and Jerry Robbins holding the floor. They're wonderful. Everything is wonderful. It's my night. I'm at the top...the very top of my game.

Once more, the creek. The taste of raw turnip on my tongue, the flow of summer water embracing my nakedness. And there, there, swiveling, tangoing on the surface, the exquisitely limber and lethal cottonmouth. But I'm not afraid, am I.

(begins to laugh, rather helplessly, then sings)

IS IT AN EARTHQUAKE, OR SIMPLY A SHOCK?
IS IT THE REAL TURTLE SOUP, OR MERELY THE MOCK?
IS IT GRANADA I SEE, OR ONLY ASBURY PARK?
OR IS IT AT LONG LAST...

(speaks) ...shit?

(Stands silently for a moment, then looks at his watch, moves toward front hall door. Pauses.)

Still. When it's time to go, shall we just ...laugh?

(He goes to stereo, turns it on. We hear Perry Como singing Little Drummer Boy,* *hurrying now,* **TRUMAN** *begins taking off his kimono as he exits through front hall door. A wait as we listen to Perry singing the haunting lyrics.)*

(Then **TRUMAN** *comes back in wearing a blazer and scarf. From upstage chair, he picks up a duffle-coat which he puts on. Then he puts on a big black borsalino, cocks it over one eye. Now he goes to lamps and turns them off, finally bends down and turns on the lights of the Christmas tree. He takes a pair of dark glasses out of his coat pocket. And puts them on. Now he picks up a big bag of presents, and holding them to his chest, stands still for a moment, looking at the tree. Then with a slight shrug, he exits.)*

(The tree lights fade but the music continues as the curtain slowly falls.)

THE END

---

*See Music Use Note on page 3.

www.ingramcontent.com/pod-product-compliance
Lightning Source LLC
Chambersburg PA
CBHW071417290426
44108CB00014B/1859